Animals at Work



# Therapy Animals

Avery Elizabeth Hurt

Enslow Publishing
101 W. 23rd Street
Suite 240
New York, NY 10011
USA
enslow.com

# Words to Know

**elderly** Old.

**emotional** Having to do with feelings.

**equipment** Items used to do a job or task.

**Humane Society** A group that works to keep animals safe.

**patient** A person who is being treated by a doctor or nurse.

**personality** The way a person or animal acts.

**pronounce** The way a word sounds when spoken.

**soothe** Make someone feel calm.

**therapy** Treatment for illness.

**veterinarian** A doctor who cares for animals.

# Contents

1

# Meet Niki

Niki meets lots of interesting people when she goes to work. People are always happy to see Niki.

Niki is a pet therapy dog. She is a six-year-old golden retriever. Her job is to visit patients in the hospital. She cheers them up. Niki is always calm and gentle. She lets people pet her. Visiting with Niki can make people feel better.

The word "therapy" means treatment for an illness. Therapy animals also help people who aren't ill. Some are worried or sad. They also help kids who have trouble paying attention. Therapy animals can't heal illnesses by themselves, but they are very good at helping doctors and nurses help people get better.

There are lots of animals like Niki. They work in many different places, not just hospitals. Therapy animals visit clinics and nursing homes. They even go to schools

Therapy animals make people feel relaxed and calm.

and libraries. Sometimes pet therapy animals visit people at home. People who are well enough to go out sometimes go to see therapy animals.

Therapy animals are not like service animals. Service animals do tasks for people. They help blind people find their way. They bring in the mail or answer the door. Therapy animals cheer people up and make them feel better. Therapy cats nap in people's

Fish are quiet and pretty. They help people feel relaxed.

## Gurgle Gurgle

**Have you ever seen a fish tank in a dentist's waiting room? Fish are therapy animals, in a way. They help calm people who are nervous about dentist visits.**

laps. People who are feeling sad take therapy dogs for short walks. Sometimes just watching animals is enough to make people feel better.

**Fact**
**Many therapy animals are rescued from animal shelters.**

Therapy pets don't go to work by themselves! Their owners take them on their visits. A therapy animal and its owner are a team. People volunteer for this special job. Then they go with their pets for special training. It feels very good to help people get better. Therapy dogs enjoy their work.

# 2

# Pets in the Lab

Animals can be good friends. Anyone who has a pet knows that. But people weren't always sure that pets could help people get well. Scientists had to do experiments to prove it.

Florence Nightingale was an English nurse in the late nineteenth century. She wrote a book about nursing. She wrote that animals could help sick people get well.

Sigmund Freud was a doctor. He helped people with emotional problems. He worked in Vienna, Austria, in the 1930s. Freud had a dog named Jofi. He often took Jofi

### Back in the Day

**Pet therapy has been around a long time. In 1752, doctors in England used pet therapy. They used rabbits and birds to help people with mental illnesses.**

Florence Nightingale lived from 1820 to 1910.

Pet rabbits love to snuggle.

with him to see patients. Jofi was very good at knowing when people were upset. He could make them feel calmer, too.

Freud and Nightingale believed that animals could help sick people get better. But they couldn't prove it. Many years later, scientists began to do experiments to find out the truth.

In 1980, scientists at a university in Pennsylvania did some research. They studied a group of people who had heart attacks. The patients who had pets got well faster. The scientists did more experiments. They discovered that petting an animal can lower a person's blood pressure. High blood pressure is a sign of many health problems. Soon lots more scientists began doing these kinds of experiments. They discovered many interesting things. Pets can help older people with memory problems. (A person who has high blood pressure for a long time can sometimes have memory

**Fact**

**Scientists also study the best ways to train pet therapy animals.**

Dogs can make you feel calm. They can also make you laugh and feel happy.

problems.) Pets can help people not worry so much. Pets can make sad people happier. Holding and petting an animal for a few minutes can make people feel better. It can make them healthier. Scientists proved that pets are good for people.

# 3

# Not Just Dogs and Cats

Do you think of dogs and cats when you think of therapy animals? Most people do. Dogs and cats are the most common pets. But many kinds of animals work as therapy pets. Horses are the second most common therapy animal! Sometimes patients ride horses. Other times they just pet them. Horses are usually very calm around people. Calm animals are perfect therapy pets.

Other therapy animals are even more surprising. A nursing home in Florida has a tortoise therapy pet.

## Mostly Dogs

**Many kind of animals are therapy animals. But dogs are still the most common.**

**Horses are big, but they can be very gentle with people.**

Her name is Shelly. (Can you guess why?) It is soothing to be around an animal as quiet as a tortoise!

Parrots are therapy pets, too. Parrots can be trained to repeat a phrase. They might say, "Everything is OK" or "You'll be fine." This can help people who are upset.

Pigs are very intelligent. They are easy to train. Pot-bellied pigs make great therapy pets.

Pet parrots like to talk to their human friends.

These two rabbits are ready to make new friends!

Betsy and Walter are rabbits. They live with their owner, Jenn. Jenn adopted Betsy and Walter from the Humane Society. The two rabbits help other people now. Jenn often takes them out in a stroller. They visit people at hospitals and schools. Walter likes to gently bump people with his head. That's how he asks people to pet him.

You probably don't think of snakes when you think of therapy animals. But they can do the job. A clinic in London, England, uses snakes to help people who are feeling sad. Even insects work as therapy animals. Taking care of crickets helps elderly people with memory problems.

**Fact**
Pet therapy animals often wear vests or badges when they are at work.

An animal doesn't have to be a dog or a cat to be a therapy pet. So many kinds of animals can be therapy pets.

# 4

# The Perfect Therapy Animal

Almost any *type* of animal can be a therapy pet. But not every pet is perfect for the job. It takes a special personality to be a therapy animal.

Therapy pets enjoy being with people. Pets that are too shy or easily frightened aren't the best therapy animals. Pets that growl and bark can't be therapy animals. Grumpy pets aren't right for the job.

Other animals are often around when therapy pets are at work. Good therapy pets don't pay attention to them. They won't try to play or fight with other animals.

## How About Your Pet?

**Want to find out if your pet could be a therapy animal? Ask a hospital or clinic in your neighborhood if there is a pet therapy program near you.**

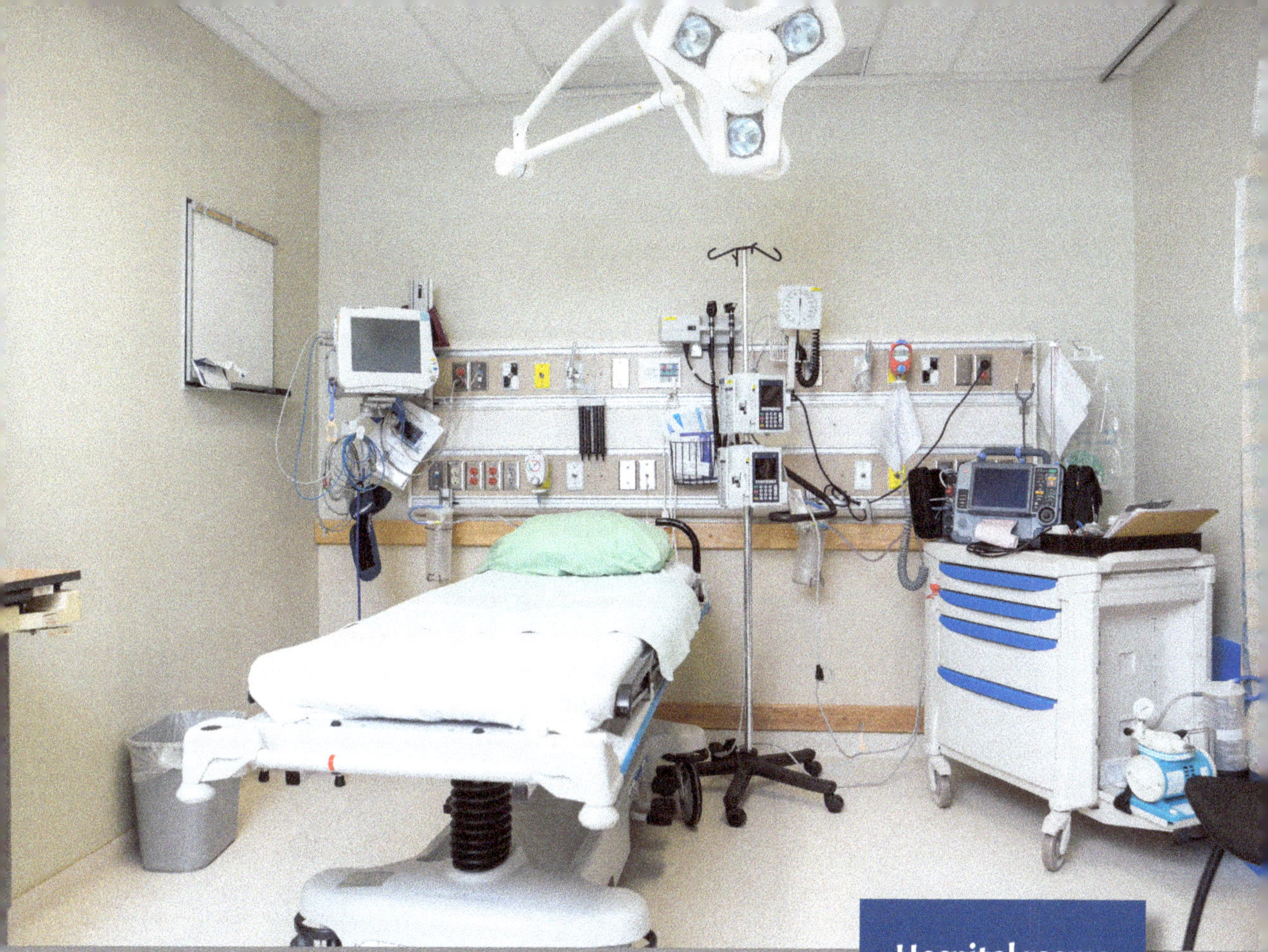

Hospital rooms can be noisy, busy places.

They don't sniff and try to get to know them.

Hospitals and medical clinics are full of strange equipment. Beds move. Machines beep. Tubes and wires snake around the rooms. Therapy pets are comfortable with all this equipment. Animals who get jumpy in strange places aren't the best therapy pets.

Therapy pets pay close attention to their human partners.

Therapy animals stay calm even when people are excited. This is especially important for therapy pets who work with kids. A good therapy pet can soothe people who are too excited. They can't do this if they get excited, too!

Good manners are very important for therapy pets. Therapy pets do not jump on people. They do not lick people. They never paw or scratch people. And of course, they don't bite anyone! Pet therapy dogs are trained to sit and stay. Lots of animals are great pets. But only special animals are great therapy pets.

**Fact**

**The United States military uses pet therapy animals to help soldiers with emotional problems.**

5

# A Team

Animals are very good at helping people feel better. But pets need help from humans, too. Humans must take care of their pets. They feed them. They make sure their pets get enough exercise. They take them to the veterinarian. And they give their pets plenty of love. If their pets are therapy animals, they help them do their jobs.

Pet owners go with their pets on therapy visits. People who help therapy pets are called handlers. The handler and the pet are called the pet therapy team. The

## Pets at Work

**Jobs that people do can be stressful. Some companies allow therapy pets to visit workers at their jobs. Therapy pets can make work less stressful.**

human is an important part of this team! Handlers are volunteers. This means that they do not get paid for their work. They do it because it is important. They like to help other people.

An animal has to be certified before it can be a therapy pet. This means an organization gets to know the animal. The organization promises that the animal has what it takes to

Fresh air and exercise keep therapy pets healthy, too.

be a therapy pet. The rules are different in some towns than in others. The rules are also different for different types of animals. Usually the animal has to be more than one year old. It must have lived with the same owner for several months.

All therapy animals get special training. Some therapy dogs take obedience classes.

**Sometimes when therapy pets go to the doctor—they are the patients!**

They must be able to follow commands like "sit" and "stay." They learn to stay calm in unfamiliar places or when they are surprised. They learn to be friendly to strangers.

**Fact**
**People who have pets have a lower risk of high blood pressure.**

Therapy pets help humans be healthy. The pets have to be healthy, too. They must get regular health checkups. They must be up to date on all their shots. And they always have to be clean and brushed. Their human handlers help them stay healthy, too.

6

# Read Me a Story

Pet therapy animals help people who are ill. But they help with other things, too. Some pet therapy animals help kids learn to read!

Have you ever read a story to your pet? If you did, your pet probably enjoyed it. And so did you. Reading to your pet can help you learn to read. This is another job of therapy pets. Here is how it works: A dog and its handler visit schools and libraries. Children get to know the dog. Then they choose a book to read to the dog. It's fun!

## Save a Life

Reading to dogs helps dogs, too. Kids read to dogs at a Missouri animal shelter. It helps shy dogs be friendlier. Friendly dogs are more likely to be adopted.

It's sometimes easier to read to a dog than to another human. Dogs don't mind if it takes a few minutes to sound out a word. They never notice if you don't pronounce a word just right. It's fun to choose a book and read it to a pet.

Reading to a dog is a good way to practice. Shy children who read to animals can get more comfortable

It's fun to read books with friends.

Playing together is good for animals and people!

talking to other people, too. It's also a good way to learn about spending time with animals.

When you read to a dog, you also get to do a lot of petting. That makes it even more fun.

**Fact**
Children who read to dogs at school read more at home, too.

Dogs, horses, pigs, cats, snakes, and insects. There are many kinds of pet therapy animals. They work in lots of places to help people. Being a therapy pet is a good job for animals at work.

# Learn More

## Books


Gavin, Jane. *Sarah and the Big Test.* Clayton, GA: Laurel Mountain Press, 2013.

Goldman, Marcia. *Lola Goes to Work: A Nine to Five Therapy Dog.* Stevens Point, WI: Creston, 2013.

Townsend, John. *Amazing Animal Helpers.* Chicago, IL: Raintree, 2015.

## Websites

### How to Love Your Dog: A Kid's Guide to Dog Care

*http://www.loveyourdog.com*

Plenty of information on caring for and training dogs. Also riddles, jokes, and other fun things.

### Science Kids: Animal Facts

*http://www.sciencekids.co.nz/sciencefacts/animals.html*

Sections on dogs and cats—and lots of other animals, too.

# INDEX




Published in 2019 by Enslow Publishing, LLC.
101 W. 23rd Street, Suite 240, New York, NY 10011





**Library of Congress Cataloging-in-Publication Data**

Names: Hurt, Avery Elizabeth, author.
Title: Therapy animals / Avery Elizabeth Hurt.
Description: New York, New York : Enslow, [2019] | Series: Animals at work | Audience: Grades 3-6. | Includes bibliographical references and index.
Identifiers: LCCN 2017053157 | ISBN 9780766096318 (library bound) | ISBN 9780766096325 (paperback) | ISBN 9780766096332 (6 pack)
Subjects: LCSH: Animals—Therapeutic use—Juvenile literature. | Working animals—Juvenile literature.
Classification: LCC RM931.A65 H87 2019 | DDC 615.8/5158—dc23
LC record available at https://lccn.loc.gov/2017053157

Printed in the United States of America





**Photo Credits:** Cover, p. 1 lucrezia senserini88/Photodisc/Getty Images; p. 5 Sergey Nivens/Shutterstock.com; p. 6 Kilian O'Sullivan/Corbis Documentary/Getty Images; p. 9 London Stereoscopic Company/Hulton Archive/Getty Images; p. 10 Anca Zahiu/Shutterstock.com; p. 12 Monkey Business Images/Shutterstock.com; p. 14 Osetrik/Shutterstock.com; p. 15 Zurijeta/Shutterstock.com; p. 16 Africa Studio/Shutterstock.com; p. 19 Tyler Olson/Shutterstock.com; p. 20 Nadezhda V. Kulagina/Shutterstock.com; p. 23 Arman Zhenikeyev/Moment/Getty Images; p. 24 Pressmaster/Shutterstock.com; p. 27 Anna Hoychuk/Shutterstock.com; p. 28 ESB Professional/Shutterstock.com.